Josiah Tucker

Reflections on the Present Matters in Dispute

Between Great Britain and Ireland

Josiah Tucker

Reflections on the Present Matters in Dispute
Between Great Britain and Ireland

ISBN/EAN: 9783337170448

Printed in Europe, USA, Canada, Australia, Japan

Cover: Foto ©Suzi / pixelio.de

More available books at **www.hansebooks.com**

REFLECTIONS

ON THE

PRESENT MATTERS IN DISPUTE

BETWEEN

Great Britain and Ireland;

AND ON THE

Means of converting these Articles into mutual Benefits to both Kingdoms.

———

By JOSIAH TUCKER, D.D.

DEAN OF GLOUCESTER.

———

LONDON:

PRINTED FOR T. CADELL, IN THE STRAND.

MDCCLXXXV.

[Price One Shilling.]

ADVERTISEMENT.

THESE papers were originally drawn up for the ufe of a few friends, who wifhed to know the Author's fentiments on a fubject which is now fo much debated in both kingdoms, and perhaps fo little underftood by the great majority in either. The requeft of my friends was, to have fome eafy clue in their enquiries, which might direct them to right conclufions, amidft the contradictory affertions, and the clafhing evidences of contending partizans. Whether the Author has been able, in the following fheets, to anfwer the expectation of his friends, is not for him to judge; but as it was their earneft requeft, that he fhould lofe no time at this critical juncture, in laying his thoughts

before

before the Public, he now fubmits them to general examination, with that deference which is due from a man, who writes for no party, is truly and literally independent of all, and wifhes no ill to any.

One thing he begs leave to add, that had he originally intended to have given thefe papers to the prefs, he would have enlarged on fome heads, which are at prefent only touched upon. He would have fhewn, in particular, from the evidence of FACTS, that a poor country, where wages are low, provifions cheap, and raw materials in the greateft plenty, has neverthelefs a manifeft difadvantage in contending with a rich one, in working up *complete* manufactures, in the price of thofe manufactures at market, the extenfion of commerce, and in fhipping and navigation. He would have

produced

produced examples of attempts having been *unfuccefsfully* made, fome of them recently, to tranfplant the woollen, the worfted, the iron and metal, the cotton, the pottery, and feveral other branches of manufacture, from richer into poorer countries; all of them having failed in a courfe of years, notwithftanding the great natural advantages belonging to the one, the poorer country, and the feeming difadvantages attending the richer. But at prefent he can only refer his readers to a tract written exprefsly on this fubject, which has ftood the teft of the moft rigorous examination as to the theoretic part, and (what is much better) which has been proved to be founded on fact and experience. The tract referred to is the firft of his Four on Political and Commercial Subjects, printed for Cadell, entituled, The Great Queftion refolved, Whether a
rich

rich country can ftand a competition with a poor country (of equal natural advantages), in raifing of provifions, and cheapnefs of manufactures ?—With fuitable inferences and deductions.

N. B. The reader, by the perufal of this tract, will immediately obferve, that every part of the reafoning, and of the facts there mentioned refpecting Scotland, conclude in a much ftronger degree in regard to Ireland.

REFLEC-

REFLECTIONS,

&c. &c. &c.

IRELAND being now an independent kingdom, is as much intitled to trade to any foreign country, as England herself:

Confequently fhe hath a right (or foon will have, when her own ill-judged act of fubjecting herfelf to the reftrictions of the Eaft India Company fhall expire) to trade to all the countries beyond the Cape of Good Hope, and particularly to Indoftan, and to China.

She has alfo a full right to trade to Egypt, and to all parts of the Mediterranean, the Archipelago, and the Levant; not to mention the Ruffian dominions bordering on the Black Sea.

B   Being

Being now no longer bound to fubmit to the Englifh monopolies of fugar, rum, &c. &c. fhe is free to refort to any market whatever for the purchafe of thefe commodities, inftead of being confined to the Englifh plantations, the deareft in the known world.

She is totally at liberty to employ whatever fhipping, Englifh or foreign, fhe may find the moft conducive to her *mercantile* intereft, for exportation, or importation of any goods or manufactures, being happily releafed from thofe burdens and impofitions on a free trade, which are contained in that famous Monopoly, called The Act of Navigation.

She is not now hampered by any Englifh laws (and it is her own fault, if fhe will hamper herfelf) relative to the exportation or importation of grain, but is at full liberty to confult the general intereft of the whole kingdom, and not the partial intereft either of the corn-grower, or of the corn-dealer.

Laftly, Ireland is not as yet infected with that ftrange phrenzy which has infected the whole Englifh nation for fo many ages, viz.
That

That all people, nations, and languages, ought to acknowledge England to be the fole miftrefs and fovereign of the feas, and to pay homage and fubmiffion to her pavilion. Ireland is hitherto untainted with that fpecies of madnefs, and confequently has provoked no other maritime power to retaliate the affront upon her.

Now all thefe fortunate circumftances, freedoms, and exemptions, might foon be made to operate to the general advantage of both kingdoms, were a judicious application to be made of felf-intereft, the ftrongeft principle in human nature. But the benefits from hence arifing, and every other benefit, muft have been furrendered up on the part of Ireland, without obtaining any other compenfation, than what was fuppofed to be contained in thofe imaginary favours, fpecified in the bill which lately paffed the Irifh Houfe of Commons; but which the Englifh merchants and manufacturers, moft happily for Ireland, have oppofed with much violence and indignation. Thefe favours may be truly ftyled *imaginary*, becaufe they are chiefly of fuch a nature, as make it impoffible

(in a commercial fenfe) for the Irifh nation
to avail itfelf of them. In fhort, they are
no equivalent for what was to be furrendered
up; and they grant nothing which can be
reduced to practice for at leaft a century to
come. On the contrary,

The FIRST MONOPOLY *to be opened for the
Benefit of both Kingdoms, will foon be a
free Trade to all the Countries beyond
the Cape of Good Hope.*

THE moft fortunate circumftance which
could have happened for Ireland is, that fhe
is hitherto unincumbered with reftrictions on
her foreign trade, unfettered by joint-ftock
companies, or exclufive privileges: confequently, as Ireland either has, or foon will
have, a free navigation from the Cape of
Good Hope to the extremities of China, there
is not a doubt to be made, but that many,
perhaps moft of thofe Englifh merchants and
manufacturers, who are the moft zealous
againft the Irifh bill, will be among the foremoft to fit out Englifh fhips and cargoes, and
to clear and victual from fome of the ports

of

of Ireland, in order to trade under the fanc-
tion of the Irifh flag. In fuch a fituation,
the face of things will be changed; no evils
will be foreboded to fall on poor Old England, even though the merchants of London,
Briftol, Liverpool, and Glafgow, and the
manufacturers of Birmingham, Manchefter,
Etruria, and Paifley, fhould fend their goods
to Arabia and Perfia, to the Eaft India and
China markets, through this *new* channel :
nor will there be any great lamentation,
fhould the returns be made in tea and china-
ware, in raw filk, cotton wool, camels hair,
ivory, drugs, indico, falt-petre, and various
other articles neceffary for the manufactures
of this kingdom. In fact, when thefe goods
and raw materials fhall be once landed in
Ireland, the neceffary confequences will foon
be felt in England : for our monopolizing
Eaft India Company will be compelled either
to lower their prices on the like articles to an
equal ftandard, or to become bankrupts.
And no honeft man, no lover of his country,
or of mankind, can truly fay, that either of
thefe alternatives would be the worft thing
that could have happened either to Afia, or
to Europe.

A SECOND MONOPOLY *to be opened for the Benefit of both Kingdoms is—A Free Trade to Egypt, the Levant, &c.*

THE fame obfervations which were made relative to the reftrictions of the Eaft India Company, may be made refpecting our Englifh Turkey Company, with this only difference, that, whereas the Eaft India Company do not fo much as pretend to grant a permiffion to any fhips to trade from any port but from the port of London, the Turkey Company, when the laft ftruggle was made for opening that trade, were obliged to grant a permiffion of a free trade in *words*, but took care to clog it with fuch difficulties as rendered it impracticable in *fact*. The Irifh nation is not bound by any of thefe reftrictive claufes; and though not capable of profiting greatly herfelf on her own ftock, yet fhe can transfer an entire freedom to any Englifh adventurer (and thereby obtain an intermediate profit to herfelf), who fhall, with a proper affortment of Englifh manufactures, clear out from fome Irifh port, and hoift the Irifh flag. Here, therefore, let it be afked,

Were

Were this to prove a lucrative branch of commerce, *who* or which among our moſt violent *Anti-Iriſh Patriots* would refuſe to ſubmit to the indignity of trading under borrowed colours?—Nay, *who*, or which of our Engliſh merchants, or manufacturers, made any ſcruple of doing the like, when the proſpect of gain was before their eyes? The writer of this paper long ago foretold, that the Engliſh and American traders would ſoon be reconciled to each other, notwithſtanding their violent and hoſtile declarations, when ſelf-intereſt became the load-ſtone of attraction. His opinion was then treated as a fooliſh paradox: The mercantile people, almoſt to a man, were pleaſed to ſcout at it; but the event has ſhewn, that he was not ſuch a dreamer, or ſo wild in his conjectures, as they imagined him to be.

A THIRD

A THIRD MONOPOLY *to be opened for the Benefit of both Kingdoms, will be— A Free Importation of Sugars, and of other Products of the warmer Climates, from the* cheapeſt Market, *wherever it can be found: and by that means a Foundation be laid for the gradual Abolition of the preſent inhuman Slave Trade.*

IT was obſerved, in the foregoing article, that ſelf-intereſt eaſily reconciles all differences, and quickly extinguiſhes national antipathies. If it went no farther, it would do no harm; nay, it would be an excellent ſuccedaneum to true and genuine benevolence. But, alas! it often goes much too far; it often ſteels the heart againſt the cleareſt convictions of honour and conſcience. In fact, the plaineſt dictate of morality, viz. Do AS YOU WOULD BE DONE BY, loſes its influence in many caſes, when oppoſed by ſelf-intereſt. There is not a man that breathes, who would approve of his being made a ſlave, in the manner that the Engliſh carry on the ſlave-trade on the coaſt of Africa, and then tranſport theſe poor wretches, to ſell them to the

Weſt

Weſt India planters. The murders commit-
ted in the courſe of this practice, reckoning
from the beginning of it to the preſent hour,
almoſt exceed the power of numbers to aſcer-
tain. Yet reaſon and humanity recoil in
vain. For the ſame trade in human blood is
ſtill carried on, not only with impunity, but
alſo with the conſent, approbation, and even
aſſiſtance of the Britiſh legiſlature. Nay, I
will venture to foretel, that the ſame will be
for ever carried on, till ſome other method
can be deviſed for ſupplying Europe with
ſugars, and with other produce of the ſouthern
climates, at a *cheaper rate* than what we receive through the medium of ſlavery. *Cheap-
neſs* alone would work a ſurpriſing alteration
in the thoughts and diſpoſitions of mankind
on ſuch ſubjects. For ſelf-intereſt (which in
the preſent caſe is only another name for *buy-
ing cheap*) would do more towards exciting
a ſtrong averſion to the preſent monopoly of
labour in our plantations, and to an abhor-
rence of the various cruelties attendant on
ſlavery, than all the reaſonings, moral argu-
ments, or eloquence in the world. Therefore, as lowering the price of ſugars, rum,
cotton, &c. &c. is the grand object to be at-

C   tended

tended to, let us fee whether the prefent ftate of Ireland can afford us any profpect towards attaining this important end. That is, whether the independence of that kingdom can, or cannot be made fubfervient to the caufe of humanity, by being ufed as a means for procuring fugars, &c. cheaper at an European market, than otherwife they would have been.

One thing is fo notorious, that it cannot be denied, viz. That the Englifh planters in general (doubtlefs there are exceptions) treat their flaves, or fuffer them to be treated, with a greater degree of inhumanity than the planters of any other European nation. The reafon of which excefs of barbarity is too eafily accounted for. As, 1ft, The Englifh planters in general have greater numbers of flaves on their plantations than others have; and the greater the number, the more feverity muft be ufed to keep them in awe, and to prevent them from combining together in favour of that paffion for liberty, which nature has implanted in every breaft. 2dly, The Englifh planters are more their own mafters, their own law-givers in their affemblies; alfo

4 the

the interpreters, the judges (as jurymen), and the executioners of their laws, than those of any other nation. The very form of the English constitution, originally calculated for the preservation of liberty, tends, in this instance, to destroy it. Consequently the English planters can indulge themselves in a greater degree of passion and revenge, than would be permitted under the absolute governments of France, Spain, Portugal, or Denmark. [See particularly the Code Noir of France. Moreover the regulations of the Spanish government respecting negroe slaves, are still more humane, laying a foundation for the sober and industrious among them, by allowing them the profits of two days labour in each week, to purchase their own liberty in the course of a few years. And it may be observed in general, that though absolute governments are tyrannical themselves, yet they are a great check on the tyranny of their intermediate subjects; being ready to protect the helpless from being oppressed by any but themselves. This is remarkably verified in the case of those slaves who live under the Russian, Prussian, and Austrian governments, compared with the

C 2.   hard

hard fate of others, who ftill groan under the bondage of the nobles of Poland.]   3dly, Many of the Englifh planters conftantly refide in England, and therefore confign the care of their eftates to thofe tyrants at fecond hand, called bailiffs or overfeers.   Now this race of mortals hath a ftronger intereft than any others, to ftifle all complaints againft them- felves, and to keep their principals as much in the dark as poffible, refpecting the ma- nagement and profits of their own eftates. Add to this, 4thly, That the planters them- felves, knowing that they have a monopoly againft the mother country, becaufe we are not permitted to refort to any other market, will keep up the price of fugars, and of the other produce of their own lands, as high as poffible: at the fame time, that they do not think themfelves bound to purchafe corn, pro- vifion, or any other merchandize at an Eng- lifh market, if they can buy the like articles cheaper in America, or any where elfe.

From all thefe circumftances, no man can be at a lofs to know the true reafon, how it comes to pafs, that the fugars, and other produce of the Britifh planters, are much dearer than, thofe

thofe of any other nation; notwithftanding that our planters have many advantages in the purchafe of their negroes, of their boilers, their mills, and of various utenfils, which others have not.

But the matter of *fact* puts this affair beyond the poffibility of a doubt. For while the common price of fugars in the Britifh iflands, in times of peace, is generally found to be about 25 fhillings fterling the Cwt.—that of the French is about 16 fhillings—that of the Portuguefe about 12 fhillings—and that of the Eaft Indies, as I have been credibly informed, no more than two fhillings and fixpence;—being, N. B. raifed or manufactured by *freemen only*.

Now, though the inhabitants of Great Britain are tied down at prefent to fuch exorbitant prices, as the monopolifing planter or his agent fhall be pleafed to extort from them; the inhabitants of Ireland are totally free, and may at any time refort to the cheapeft market: confequently, by a judicious ufe and application of this freedom, they may become the means, not only of emancipating the un-

happy

happy natives of Guinea fom their prefent galling yoke (though I own, by flow and almoft imperceptible degrees), but may alfo convince mankind in general of the momentous truth, not yet thoroughly underftood, That of all monopolies, flavery is the moft prejudicial to the true interefts of a trading nation.

Suppofe, therefore, that fhips were fitted out from Cork, or Waterford, or from any other Irifh port, with cargoes of Englifh manufactures (becaufe the Englifh are by far the beft and cheapeft that can be got, and may be procured on the *longeft* credit),· and properly forted for the French, Spanifh, Portuguefe, Danifh, or Dutch Plantations; or indeed for any of the newly erected *free ports* in thofe feas; in that cafe, is there a doubt to be made, but that the Englifh merchants and manufacturers, with their large capitals, would be the principal adventurers? and can you imagine that the difference in the refpective prices between 25 *s.* 16 *s.* and 12 *s.* *per* Cwt. would not be a ftrong temptation to them to make the trial? not to mention the additional circumftance arifing from the greater

greater profits to be made on the fale of the manufactures or outfets, when fent to thefe *new* markets.

But this is not all : for if the fugars raifed by flaves in the French, and other iflands, where flavery is of the milder kind, are much cheaper than thofe which are raifed in our Englifh plantations, the fugars which *free-men* cultivate in the Eaft Indies (working on their own account), are by far the cheapeft of all. An evident proof this, that the cheapnefs of manufactures is to be obtained by freedom only, and not by the chains and fetters, ftripes and lafhes, of the labourers employed therein !

Now, laying all thefe circumftances toge-ther, no man can be fo blind, but he muft fee, that the principles of morality, and of national commerce, agree in this refpect in perfect harmony ; and therefore, that in proportion as fuch fyftems of freedom, and of humanity, fhall gain ground, in the fame proportion will every planter, or fugar-grower, be compelled, by the neceffity of the cafe, to lighten the yoke from off the necks of his flaves, and to emancipate them by
little

little and little, till at laft a general revolu-
tion will enfue (as was, N. B. formerly the
cafe here in England), and flavery be no
more.

Moreover, to facilitate this good work, let
it be further obferved, that the fugar-cane
grows fpontaneoufly, and that rice, cotton,
indico, and other articles of great value, may
be raifed with very little trouble in thofe
parts of Africa, from whence the flaves are
ufually imported. What, therefore, remains
to be done for the completion of this good
work, but to point out to the inhabitants of
thefe regions fuch circumftances, wherein
their own advantage and commercial interefts do properly confift? and to prove to
them, by obvious facts, that they will get
more by manufacturing the fugar-cane at
home, and by raifing rice, indico, cotton, co-
chineal, &c. &c. on their own lands, than
they can receive by trucking for their own
flefh and blood, their fons and their daugh-
ters, or by making wars on their innocent
neighbours, in order to fell their prifoners for
flaves, fome thoufands of miles from their
native homes? If any thing more could be
added,

added, to caufe them to feel the horror and
iniquity of fuch proceedings, it fhould be
this, to inform them, that one-third at leaft
of thefe unhappy victims die in their paffages,
and of the difeafes contracted on board the
fhips, by being ftowed fo clofe together : that
one-third more are generally loft by the fea-
foning of the climate ; and that the remainder
linger out a wretched life, till *that* death,
which has been fo often wifhed for, fhall re-
leafe them from their mifery.

Be it therefore remembered, and be it duly
attended to, that thefe, and many other evils,
may be totally prevented by the methods
here propofed. Be it, I fay, never to be for-
gotten (at leaft for the fake of felf-intereft, if
not for better motives), that in a courfe of
years, perhaps in little more than half a century, not only Great Britain and Ireland, but
alfo all Europe, may be fupplied (if they
pleafe), with fugars, and all the products of
the warmer climates, without flavery, without colonies, without governments and place-
men, without fees and perquifites, without
forts and guarda-coftas, without contracts,
and without jobbs.

D   *A* FOURTH

A FOURTH MONOPOLY *to be opened for the Benefit of both Kingdoms, will be a free Navigation, exempted from those Clogs and Restrictions which are required by the famous Act of Navigation.*

THE precise idea of a Monopoly is this, that it is a privilege, or exclusive charter granted to serve a *few*, at the expence, and to the detriment of the *many*. According to this definition, it is impossible that *that* famous Monopoly, called The Act of Navigation, can be vindicated on the footing of *commercial* utility. National prejudices, indeed, are strongly in its favour; but prejudice and reason are not always the same thing; and it doth not follow that nations, any more than individuals, have ever been infallible in their judgments, or have consulted their own interests in the course of their proceedings: England alone can furnish examples without number of this melancholy truth. This being premised, we have two points now to consider, viz. 1st, Whether it can be for the *benefit* of the public in general (abstracted from any *particular* consideration),

that

that the landed and trading interests should be circumscribed, or limited by a monopoly in the freight, carriage, or transport of their own goods and merchandize? and then, 2dly, Whether the excuses usually brought for making this sacrifice, namely, *that it increases the breed of seamen*, hath a just foundation in fact, or can be warranted by experience? The discussion of which two questions will, it is apprehended, contain the whole substance of what can be said on this subject; I mean, as far as reason and argument are to have any share therein. Now, respecting the first inquiry, if any doubt can be started on this head, it must be this, that mankind in general have not the same sense to judge of what is, or is not for their own *immediate* advantage in this case, as they have in all others; and therefore ought to be subject to the restraints of tutors and guardians, to prescribe terms for the regulation of their conduct. But as this is a proposition too glaringly false, and too absurd to be seriously maintained, recourse must therefore be had to the second point, namely, That the great body of the people must be abridged of their natural rights and liberties of employing whomsoever they

please,

pleafe, *for the fake of keeping up, and encreaf-*
ing the number of failors to man our navy.
Now, this is the firft inftance which oc-
curs in hiftory, of monopolies and reftraint
being judged to be a proper mode of multiplying the numbers of perfons employed in
the conduct and execution of them. The
ufual train of reafoning hath been quite the
reverfe : however, to give the matter a fair
hearing, let us try the effects of the prefent
Monopoly, in a cafe of which every man is
a competent judge, and which is exactly pa-
rallel to this before us.

A merchant-fhip is nothing more than a
fea-waggon for the exportation and importation of its lading; the ufe of which is corre-
fpondent to the carriage or re-carriage of
goods by land-waggons. Or, to come ftill
clofer to the point, it anfwers the idea of the
freight, both forwards and backwards, of
wares and merchandize fent along our navi-
gable rivers, and inland canals. Now, can
any man be fo loft to common fenfe, as to
maintain, that were exclufive patents to be
granted either to our waggons by land, or
to our barges and trows by water, this would
be

be a means of multiplying the number of
thofe who fhould be employed on either ele-
ment? And yet this he muft maintain, and
prove likewife, before he can juftify the act of
navigation, as a proper meafure for encreafing
the breed of failors. The only rational and
effectual method of encreafing the numbers
to be employed either by land or water, is to
encreafe the quantity of produce, of raw materials, and of all kinds of bulky manufactures, which require to be conveyed from
place to place. For thefe will of courfe create
a demand for more waggons, more trows,
barges, and veffels for the carriage or tranf-
portation of them, than otherwife would have
been neceffary. Whereas, to begin with
fchemes to increafe the number of waggons,
or quantity of fhipping, without having a
prior regard, or without giving due encouragement to encreafe the quantity of goods to
be carried, is furely to begin at the wrong
end; and, as the old proverb expreffes it, to
put the cart before the horfe. In fact, every
thing in trade ought to be left to find its own
level; and no monopoly, or exclufive privilege, ought to be granted to one fet of
traders in preference to another. When the
fea-

sea-carrier finds that he is encouraged, and, as it were, exhorted by means of an exclusive privilege, to raise his price of freight, as having no rivals to contend with, can it be supposed that he will not avail himself of this circumstance? Or, is there an instance to be produced of any number of men, when knit together, and united by a legal monopoly, who sacrificed their own interest to that of the Public? Whereas emulation between rival carriers, rival merchants, and rival manufacturers of every sort and kind, operates by a ratio just the reverse. The price of freight, of goods, merchandize, labour, wages, and provisions, is then reduced to its just standard. And every individual, by striving to outdo his neighbour, and to get the most custom, serves the Public by his endeavours to serve himself. This has ever been the fact, and ever will be, according to the reason and nature of things. Now, as far as the encrease of shipping, and consequently of sailors, is concerned, one example, and a *striking* one it is, may serve instead of a thousand. Since the peace has been concluded with America, our trade between Great Britain and the American continent hath greatly encreased. And

what

what hath been the confequence? More Englifh fhipping, and *larger* fhips (I fay *Englifh*,
not American), have been employed in that
fervice, than ever were employed during the
fame fpace of time before. Now, this I aver
has been the fact, notwithftanding the act of
navigation itfelf has been fuperfeded in favour
of thefe revolted colonies; and every indul-
gence hath been fhewn to them, which hath
been hitherto denied to other nations, though
they moft certainly have a better claim.

However, an opening is now made: and
in the prefent enlightened ftate of things, fuch
an affair. as this cannot recede, but muft go
forward. Other nations will think themfelves extremely ill-ufed (and with great
juftice) unlefs they, our friends and beft cuftomers, fhall be put on an equal footing with
the Americans, fo lately our bittereft enemies,
and at prefent far, very far from being our
moft punctual paymafters, or beft cuftomers.

But above all, the independence of Ireland
will neceffarily give a *coup de grace* to this
injurious monopoly, as well as to feveral
others. The Irifh are not bound by our act

5   of

of navigation, or by any other of our reftrain-
ing laws. They are therefore at full liberty
to employ what fhipping they may find the
moft conducive to their own intereft; and the
Englifh adventurers, who will have the chief
fhare in the fitting out of fuch fhips and
cargoes, will rejoice to find, that they enjoy
that liberty in the ports of Ireland, which is
denied to them in their own. At laft, indeed, the Englifh legiflature itfelf will grow
wifer by experience, and learn, from the example before their eyes, that trade ought not
to be circumfcribed, and that the beft and
fureft means of encouraging the breed of
failors, is to encourage the cheapnefs of freight,
and to promote rivalfhip and emulation among
all ranks and claffes in fociety, more efpecially
among the commercial.

A FIFTH

A FIFTH MONOPOLY *to be opened for the Benefit of both Kingdoms, will confift in the free Exportation and Importation of Grain.*

WHEN men fet out wrong in any fcheme, the farther they proceed, the more diftant they are from the right courfe. This hath been remarkably verified in the regulations, which have obtained the confent of the legiflature refpecting the exportation and importation of corn.

Corn is a *raw material*, in the moft extenfive fenfe of the word. Confequently every encouragement which ought to be given for encreafing the quantity of any material, the moft neceffary and ufeful, and for which there is a never-ceafing demand, ought to be given to the growth of corn at home, and for the importation of it from abroad.

The moft proper method for encouraging the growth of corn at home, is to multiply the number of inhabitants and eaters of bread. The moft effectual way of doing this,

E   is,

is, to render the means of fubfiftence fo eafy and comfortable, that the common people may not find the weight of an encreafing family a burden too heavy for them to bear. Population will then be the neceffary confequence. This is the order of Providence. The proper method for encouraging the importation of corn from abroad, is to admit the unconditional importation of it at all times and feafons, without any reftraint or limitation whatfoever.

But corn is not only a raw material, the increafe whereof is in that fenfe, and on that account to be encouraged, but it is alfo a material of a perifhable nature, which daily grows worfe by keeping. Therefore it ought to be exported, whilft it remains good and wholefome; otherwife the vender will be a great lofer, and the eater of fuch bread, if he can eat it, will be materially injured.

For thefe reafons, were there no others, it is very evident that the exportation of corn ought never to be reftrained, unlefs under fuch an unhappy and uncommon circumftance, where crops have failed in every other country,

country, and a general famine is likely to enfue. As to the importation of it, it is abfurd
to fuppofe, that any raw material, and more
efpecially the moft momentous of all others,
fhould be prohibited from being brought in,
and the ufes of it reftrained, for the fake of
enriching a few monopolizers.

Thefe points being admitted, it becomes a
matter of aftonifhment to the unbiaffed en-
quirer after truth, how it comes to pafs, that,
in fo plain a cafe, men of judgment and re-
flection could mifs the right path, and be
continually deviating in error. But, alas!
thofe of the greateft fagacity and difcernment
are as eafily fwayed by the confideration of
profit and *lofs*, as any others; and are, therefore, too generally blind to any thing refpecting the public good, if in oppofition to their
own immediate intereft. This is a melancholy truth, which needs no illuftration. All
the corn laws now in being, were formed on
one and the fame general principle, viz. That
the good of the whole was to be facrificed to
the interefts of particular monopolizers: and
the feveral alterations, explanations, or fuppofed amendments which have been made

from

from time to time, were evidently not intended to go to the root of the evil, but to temporife; fo that the opportunities of committing frauds by one fet of men, fhould, for the future, be transferred to that of another.

The bill new depending (April 1785), propofes to reftrain the abufes, or fuppofed abufes, faid to be practifed by the exporters or importers of corn, belonging to thofe parts of the kingdom which are far diftant from the metropolis. A good hearing this! But what is the cure of the evil, and the remedy propofed? Why truly, that the exporters and importers belonging to the port of London, fhall have an exclufive right of committing the like frauds for the future; and that the price of corn in all other parts of the kingdom, as to exports and imports, fhall be regulated by the price, or fuppofed price of the London market. A moft patriotic method! and likely to do much good! Yet when the matter is traced to its confequences, this propofed amendment of the prefent evil will turn out to be nothing better than as here reprefented, viz. an artful fcheme for engroffing the whole trade of the kingdom, relative to

the

the export or import of corn, into the hands of a dozen, or a fcore-of over-grown corn-factors, belonging to the capital. Indeed the very idea of opening or of fhutting the port of London, or of any other port, according as the private intereft of thofe individuals, who are engaged in the corn-trade, fhall fuggeft, is fufficient to explain the whole myftery, and to account for that uncommon zeal, which is difplayed on either fide in this controverfy. As to the folemnity of an oath (which is always 'required), we know but too weil, from fatal experience, that this is not to be relied upon, becaufe it is but a feeble barrier againft the temptation of felf-intereft, and the pro-fpect of greater gain; and where a profecution for perjury is in a manner impoffible.

Put the cafe, that the corn-factor, whether in London, or any other fea-port town, it matters not, has either a great ftock in his own warehoufes, or has engaged the corn-growers in the adjacent counties under con-tract, to fupply him with large quantities at a *certain price*. In either cafe it is manifeftly his intereft to fhut up the ports againft im-ports, in order that he may fell at an higher price,

price, and prevent any foreign corn from rivaling him at market. Therefore he contrives ways and means, at the cheap expence of a few oaths, to get the ports clofed up by law, till his ftcck can be fold off: and if you can believe him, he has no other view in fo doing, than to promote the *landed interefi*, and to alleviate the burdens under which they now groan. But when the quantity of his ftores are confiderably leffened, then he changes his note, and having received intelligence from his agents abroad, that ladings are fecured, and his fhips ready to fail, then he feels (though not before) for the diftreffes of the manufacturing poor (the landed interefl being at that juncture to be forgot); and he applies for opening the ports, by the very fame methods which had been ufed for fhutting them before. But when his cargoes are fafely landed, and his ftorehoufes are filled, the ports are to be fhut again, and the landed interefl is to be again promoted,—till the prefent ftock fhall be fold off,—and thus the farce goes round; in which, while public good is the cry, private interefl is the real mover behind the fcenes. Indeed, I do not fay but that both may fometimes coincide. But

But it is evident from the tenor of the present bill, and from the frauds which are said to have been detected in the whole business both of exports and imports, that the system itself, which administers such continual temptations to fraud and chicane, and even bare-faced perjury, must be totally wrong, and that no cure can be administered, but that which is radical, viz. A general permission both for the exportation and importation of grain at all times and seasons, and to and from all places. And till this is done, much may be pretended, while little is effected. London may accuse the out-ports, and the out-ports may retort the accusation. But every disinterested, impartial man must be obliged to confess, that there is too much truth in the criminations and recriminations on both sides, and that to each of them it may be truly said, *Thou art the man.*

The writer of this paper will not pay so bad a compliment to the intellects of any of his readers, as to suppose them not convinced, that the present corn-laws ought to be in a manner totally changed; and that, if the general good was to be the point to be consulted, both the exportation and importation

tion of corn ought to be left to take their
own free courfe, without any interference
of the legiflature. But, alas! when felf-intereft holds the balance, reafon, and convic-
tion, and the public good, are too often found
to be *trifles light as air.* He doth not therefore depend on the ftrength of his argument
for the fuccefs of this caufe.

The independence of Ireland is his fheet-
anchor in this refpect, as well as in the for-
mer: for when the corn-trade between North
America and Ireland (together with fome
other articles connected with and dependent
on it) fhall be left to fettle itfelf into a
fyftem; then the Britifh corn-factors, when
prohibited from importing into Great Britain,
will certainly import into fome of the weftern
or northern ports of Ireland, if they fhall
find it their intereft fo to do; provided the
Irifh will have the good fenfe to give them
leave. Ireland will thereby become a kind of
magazine or granary for the middle and fouth-
ern parts of Europe; fo that the fcarcity of
one country will be fupplied by the fuper-
abundance of another. This will awaken the
attention, and excite the jealoufy and emulation of Great Britain; and then the Englifh

traders

traders themfelves will be among the foremoft to apply for a repeal of all thefe monopolizing laws, when they fhall find that they can no longer make any ufe of them to their own private advantage, but, on the contrary, that this monopolizing fyftem will neceffarily operate to the benefit of their rivals.

Upon the whole, it is evidently for the intereft of both kingdoms, that the prefent bill fhould be deferred. Matters are not yet ripe enough for either country to avail itfelf of thofe advantages, which may be enjoyed on both fides in the courfe of ten or fifteen years hence, were every thing till then to remain *in ftatu quo* ; and were the confideration of the whole affair to be poftponed to that diftant period. New lights would then arife ; new interefts and connections would be formed ; and it is not improbable, but that the moft violent oppofers of a *real union*, would be then the moft zealous to promote it. At prefent, an alliance, fuch as is propofed by the bill now depending, may be truly faid to hang out falfe colours to both nations : for it buoys the Irifh up with delufive hopes, which cannot be realized according to the fyftem now propofed ; and it fills the Englifh with terrors and

F   panics,

panics, which have no foundation but in the artifice of the *few*, and the credulity of the *many*. Happily for the world, it is the prerogative of Providence to bring good out of evil. This may be clearly feen in a thoufand inftances ; and it will be our faults (I include the Irifh, as well as Englifh), if we do not turn to our own profit and advantage the evil which is now before us.

A real union and incorporation with Ireland is certainly a moft defirable thing; but, according to the prefent fituation of affairs, and men's tempers and difpofitions, this is an event more to be wifhed for, than to be expected. Neverthelefs, when many of thofe obftacles, which now appear fo formidable, fhall be fmoothed by the lenient hand of time, and when a mutual intercourfe between England and Ireland (according as above defcribed) fhall confer mutual benefits on each other; it will then be found, that the only thing remaining towards completing the commercial and political fyftem, and towards giving ftrength and fecurity, confiftence and ftability to the whole, will be to unite under one legiflature, to form one parliament, and to become ONE PEOPLE.

A P-

Subjects for Differtations and Per-
miums, to be offered to the GRA-
DUATE STUDENTS of the UNIVER-
SITIES of ENGLAND and SCOTLAND,

Written December 1784.

IT is a juft complaint, and hath been of long
ftanding, that the general tenor of acade-
mical ftudies hath very little tendency towards
inftructing the rifing generation in the civil,
political, and commercial interefts of their
own country, when they come abroad into
the world, and are to take fome active part
on the ftage of life. On the contrary, it is
obfervable, that a young gentleman may even
excel in almoft every one of thofe exercifes,
which are either required of him for his pub-

F 2   lic

lic degrees, or prefcribed by his tutor for private inftruction; and yet be very deficient in
that kind of knowledge, which is neceffary to
form the public-fpirited citizen, the enlightened fenator, and the real patriot; and, what is
ftill worfe, the greater his zeal, without fuch
knowledge, the more liable he will be to pur-
fue wrong meafures, injurious to his country
and to mankind, though with the beft inten-
tions of doing what is right.

To remedy thefe inconveniences, at leaft in
part, the following propofals are humbly fub-
mitted to the judgment of the Public—The
Author himfelf hath been long of the opinion,
that the fubjects here propofed, or fome others
of the fame tendency, are proper for inftructing young men of letters of every denomi-
nation, in the real interefts and true policy,
not only of Great-Britain, but of all the
nations upon earth. But as he makes no
pretenfions to infallibility, he fhall await the
public decifion, with that deference and refpect which duty enjoins, and decency re-
quires; happy in the confcioufnefs of his own
mind, of having meant the *beft*.

FIRST

FIRST SUBJECT.

Whether a ſtrict attention to agriculture and manufactures, and to their inſeparable concomitant, a free, extended, and national commerce, can be made compatible with a ſpirit of heroiſm, and great military glory? and in caſe there ſhould be found an incongruity between them, which ought to have the preference?—conqueſts, colonies, and a widely extended empire? or, domeſtic induſtry and frugality, a free trade, and great internal population?

SECOND SUBJECT.

What *kind*, and *quantity* of military force ſeem to be ſufficient for guarding, from foreign invaſion, or domeſtic robbery, the agriculture and manufactures, the ſhipping and commerce of *that particular country*, whoſe ſole aim is to excel in the arts of peace, without attempting to give laws to other nations, or to exult over them either by land or ſea, and not pretending to regulate the balance of power between the contending nations of the world?

THIRD

THIRD SUBJECT.

Whether an examination into the nature of the above fubjects doth or doth not lead to conclufions favourable to the interefts of this country in particular, and to the good of mankind in general? And if it fhould be found to be favourable to the good of *all*, whether a fyftem of politics and commerce, built on fuch a plan, would promote or dif-courage the employing of *flaves* inftead of hiring *free men*, for the purpofes of agriculture, manufacture, and national commerce?

FOURTH SUBJECT.

In cafe it fhould be found, on due examination, that flavery is repugnant not only to humanity, but alfo to the general interefts of agriculture, manufactures, and national commerce,—Quere, What methods ought to be devifed for fupplying Great Britain with fugars, and other productions of the Weft Indies, which are now raifed by flaves only? and how might fuch a benevolent fcheme be carried into execution by gentle means, fure

and

and progreffive in their operation, but free
from violence?

FIFTH SUBJECT.

Suppofing fuch alterations in the commercial fyftem as above fuggefted, and ac-
companied by the *revocation of all monopolies
whatever*—would fuch a fcheme, if put in
practice, be attended with any additional
expence to government? would it obftruct
the collection of the feveral duties and taxes
at home? or would it be any impediment to
the protection of our trade abroad? and, above
all, would it tend to the accumulation, or di-
minution of the burden of the prefent enor-
mous national debt?

R O P O S E D,

That 200 l. be raifed by fubfcription for
giving premiums to the *graduate* ftudents of
the univerfities of England and Scotland, for
the beft Englifh differtations (if deferving
to appear in print) on *one*, or *more* of the
above mentioned fubjects, namely,

IN

IN ENGLAND.

£

To the univerſity of Oxford, for
    the beſt diſſertation   -   £. 30
To ditto, for the ſecond beſt   20

                                    ——   5c

To the univerſity of Cambridge,
    for the beſt   -   -   30
To ditto, for the ſecond beſt   20

                                    ——   50

                                    ——
                                        100

IN SCOTLAND.

To the univerſity of Edinburgh,
    for the beſt   -   -   15
To ditto, for the ſecond beſt   10

                                    ——   25

To the univerſity of Glaſgow, for
    the beſt   -   -   15
To ditto, for the ſecond beſt   10

                                    ——   25

To the univerſity of St. Andrew's,
    for the beſt   -   -   15
To ditto, for the ſecond beſt   10

                                    ——   25

                Carried forward   £. 75

Brought forward £. 75
To the univerfities of old, and new
   Aberdeen, for the beft   -   15
To ditto, for the fecond beft   10
                           — 25

£. 100

N. B. The propofer of the above fcheme will himfelf give twenty pounds towards it; and will engage for twenty more from his friends, if found neceffary. Moreover, he will continue the fame fubfcription for life, if the public voice fhould be favourable for the continuance of fuch a fet of annual premiums.

F I N I S.